The Server's Handbook

The Alternative Service Book 1980
Rite A

Lester Yeo
Priest of the Exeter Diocese

RELIGIOUS AND MORAL EDUCATION PRESS
An Imprint of Arnold-Wheaton

Religious and Moral Education Press
An Imprint of Arnold-Wheaton
Hennock Road, Exeter EX2 8RP

A Division of E.J. Arnold & Son Ltd
Registered office at Parkside Lane, Leeds LS11 5TD

A subsidiary of Pergamon Press Ltd
Headington Hill Hall, Oxford OX3 0BW

Pergamon Press Inc.
Maxwell House, Fairview Park, Elmsford, New York 10523

Pergamon Press Canada Ltd
Suite 104, 150 Consumers Road, Willowdale, Ontario M2J 1P9

Pergamon Press (Australia) Pty Ltd
P.O. Box 544, Potts Point, N.S.W. 2011

Pergamon Press GmbH
Hammerweg 6, D-6242 Kronberg, Federal Republic of Germany

First published 1984

Printed in Great Britain by A. Wheaton & Co. Ltd, Hennock Road, Exeter

ISBN 0 08-030608-X

Contents

Acknowledgements

The text of the Eucharist on pages 15–40 of this book follows an authorized order of The Order for Holy Communion Rite A on pages 119–173 of The Alternative Service Book 1980. Some parts of the service, for example, the Eucharistic Prayers, are not reproduced in full. Material which is not part of the authorized service of Rite A has been included for the purpose of instruction of servers and personal prayer.

The Order for Holy Communion Rite A from The Alternative Service Book 1980 is © the Central Board of Finance of the Church of England and is reproduced with permission.

The collect 'Eternal God and Father...' on page 3 is from Morning Prayer and the collect 'Lighten our darkness...' on page 4 is from Evening Prayer in The Alternative Service Book 1980; both are reproduced with permission.

The extracts from Psalms 5 and 134 are from *The Psalms: A New Translation for Worship* (*The Liturgical Psalter*), © English text 1976, 1977 David L Frost, John A Emerton, Andrew A Macintosh, and are reproduced by permission of Collins Liturgical Publications.

Extracts from the New English Bible, Second Edition, Copyright © 1970, are reproduced by permission of Oxford and Cambridge University Presses.

The prayers 'Lord, I don't like being ill...' on page 6 and 'Jesus, Thank you for coming into the world...' on page 9 are from *Live and Pray*, by Brother Kenneth CGA and Sister Geraldine Dss CSA, © Community of the Glorious Ascension and Deaconess Community of St Andrew, and are reproduced by permission of CIO Publishing.

The publishers wish to thank J. Wippell & Co. Ltd, Exeter, for lending the chalice for the cover photograph.

Cover photography by Martin Chambers.

Illustrated by Oxford Illustrators.

Introduction

Servers have an important role to play in the life of the Church; because they assist the priest at the altar, more than any other lay person they are conspicuous in public worship. And yet the good server should never be noticed, because it is the action of the Eucharist that should always be the centre of the congregation's attention. There is a fine line between good serving and both careless and ostentatious serving. The only way to achieve good serving is for it to be an outward expression of love for Christ, who is the centre of our faith.

Therefore being a server is not simply a matter of helping the priest in the sanctuary. Being a server involves a relationship with Christ, a relationship that must be nurtured by regular attendance at the Eucharist whether serving or not, by personal prayer and Bible reading, and by a Christian lifestyle, typified by love and concern and Christ-like simplicity. As a result this book, as well as containing the text of the Eucharist with serving instructions, and information of use to the server, also contains a collection of prayers and a preparation for communion to help strengthen that relationship.

Note

When Denis Taylor wrote *Serving at the Altar* in 1966, all churches with servers used much the same ceremonial, and the service was normally from the Book of Common Prayer. Only in the last twenty years have the effects of the liturgical movement really been felt in parishes throughout the country. The Eucharist is now commonly celebrated with the priest facing the people, and in many buildings the altar has been moved into the body of the church. The publication of The Alternative Service Book 1980 has given the Church of England in Rite A a standard liturgy in modern English. These factors mean that it is no longer possible to write about serving with any of the certainty of *Serving at the Altar*. In this book, the serving instructions are of a more general kind, and it is hoped that they will conform with the practice of most Anglican parishes.

PART 1

Praying Every Day

It is the duty and the joy of the Christian to pray regularly and to spend some time in quietness with God. Praying is simple but it is not easy; using set words and written prayers can help but may also mean very little to us; using our own words, or indeed no words at all, may on the other hand mean we pray only for our own concerns, and may allow our minds to wander. Distracting thoughts are bound to invade our prayers. Don't worry. When this happens, make an effort to go back to the point in your prayers where your thoughts started to wander.

The clergy and many lay people use the Prayer of the Church, the services of Morning and Evening Prayer, to provide a structure for their prayer life. A simple form of daily prayer, such as that given below, may be useful for all Christians as a springboard for our communication with God. If you use this form of prayer, there is room for your own personal prayers before the Lord's Prayer. Make a list of the people close to you and all who may need your prayers; work out for whom you intend to pray each day. In the evening, thank God for the good things that have happened during the day, then remember your sins and tell God that you are sorry.

IN THE MORNING

O Lord, open my lips
  and my mouth shall proclaim your praise.

Psalm 5
In the morning when I pray to you,
surely you will hear my voice:
  at daybreak I lay my prayers before you, and look up.
But let all who put their trust in you rejoice:
  let them shout with joy for ever.
Be the defender of those who love your name:
  let them exult because of you.
Glory to the Father and to the Son:
  and to the Holy Spirit;
as it was in the beginning, is now:
  and shall be for ever. Amen.

Praise be to the God and Father of our Lord Jesus Christ who in his great mercy gave us new birth into a living hope by the resurrection of Jesus Christ from the dead. *(1 Peter 1: 3)*

Our Father...

Eternal God and Father,
you create us by your power
and redeem us by your love;
guide and strengthen us by your Spirit,
that we may give ourselves in love and service
to one another and to you;
through Jesus Christ our Lord. Amen.

May the Lord bless us and keep us from all evil,
and bring us to eternal life. Amen.

IN THE EVENING

O Lord, open my lips
    and my mouth shall proclaim your praise.

Psalm 134
Come bless the Lord,
all you servants of the Lord:
    you that by night stand
    in the house of our God.
Lift up your hands toward the holy place
and bless the Lord:
    may the Lord bless you from Zion,
    the Lord who made heaven and earth.
Glory to the Father and to the Son:
    and to the Holy Spirit;
as it was in the beginning, is now:
    and shall be for ever. Amen.

It is not ourselves that we proclaim, we proclaim Christ Jesus as Lord, and ourselves as your servants, for Jesus' sake. For the same God who said, 'Out of darkness let light shine,' has caused his light to shine within us, to give the light of revelation – the revelation of the glory of God in the face of Jesus Christ.

(2 Corinthians 4: 5–6)

Father,
I am sorry that I have sinned against you;
forgive me and help me live
   to the glory of your name;
for the sake of Jesus Christ your Son our Lord. Amen.

Our Father...

Lighten our darkness, Lord, we pray;
and in your mercy defend us
from all perils and dangers of this night;
for the love of your only Son,
our Saviour Jesus Christ. Amen.

May the Lord bless us and keep us from all evil,
and bring us to eternal life. Amen.

Prayers

Devotional Prayers
I hand over to your care, Lord,
My soul and body
My mind and thoughts
My prayers and my hopes
My health and my work
My life and my death
My parents and my family
My friends and my neighbours
My country and all men
Today
And always.

(Launcelot Andrewes)

Father,
you love everything that makes people free to serve you.
Real peace comes from you.
For when we do what you want
we know your presence,
and are at peace with our neighbours,
and with ourselves.

And, Father,
when I am not at peace with myself,
when my body wants to break your laws,
   when it has,
   and I have a guilty conscience –
help me not to rely on myself
but on you;
and when I lose,
may your Holy Spirit remind me
that Jesus wasn't defeated in the end.

(Based on a prayer by Thomas Cranmer)

Father,
   you help us to understand you
   you give life to those who love you
   and your strength to those who want to serve you
Help me
   to understand more about you
   – that I may love you more
   to love you so much
   – that I may serve you better
For I know that to obey you
   is not slavery
   but real freedom.

(Based on a prayer by St Augustine)

Lord, make me an instrument of your peace.
Where there is hatred, let me sow love;
where there is injury, let there be pardon;
where there is discord, union;
where there is doubt, faith;
where there is despair, hope;
where there is darkness, light;
where there is sadness, joy;
for your mercy and for your truth's sake. Amen.

(Commonly ascribed to St Francis of Assisi)

Jesus,
thank you
for all the good things
you have given me,
for all the pain and insults
you took in my place.
Most merciful Lord
   my Redeemer
   my friend
   my brother,
may I
   know you more clearly
   love you more dearly
   follow you more nearly
for no other reason
except your love for me.

(Based on a prayer by St Richard of Chichester)

Teach us, Lord, how to follow you,
   how to give help
   without expecting anything in return:
   how to stick up for what we believe
   even when others jeer at us:
   how to do your work in the world
   and not get tired of doing it.
   How to be *real* Christians,
just because this is what you want us to be
and not because we hope to be praised for it.

(Based on a prayer by St Ignatius of Loyola)

When Ill
Lord,
I don't like being ill –
give me patience.
Stop me complaining
and help me to pray for others who are sick.

(Br Kenneth CGA and Sr Geraldine Dss CSA)

For the Church
Father
we pray for your Church.
Fill it with your truth and your peace.
Where it is in error, correct it;
where it is right, strengthen it;
where it is in need, provide for it;
where it is divided, heal it and unite it in your love.

(Based on a prayer by William Laud)

For Servers and Others
Lord,
strengthen for service the hands which have held holy things;
may the ears which have heard your word be deaf to the noise of
    disputes;
may the tongues which have sung your praise never lie;
may the eyes which have seen the signs of your love shine with hope;
and may the bodies which have been fed with your body be made new
    by your risen life.

(Based on a prayer from the liturgy of Malabar)

For Those in Authority
Father,
bless those whom I love and who love me;
    those who have helped me in my life;
    those in authority over me in Church or government (or school);
    those under my care or under my influence;
I ask this for Jesus' sake.

(Based on a prayer by Dean Vaughan)

For Peace
Father,
lead me from death to life, from falsehood to truth;
lead me from despair to hope, from fear to trust;
lead me from hate to love, from war to peace;
let peace fill our heart, our world, our universe;
for your Son is the Prince of Peace, Jesus Christ, our Lord.

For Friends and Relations
Lord,
the Holy Spirit has given us the gift of love;
give health in body and soul to those we love,
so that they may love you more and more,
and be happy in following you.

(Based on a prayer from the Gregorian sacramentary)

For Those in Need and the Ill
Father,
your love goes on for ever and you do not forget the sufferings of this world – the needs of the homeless; the cry of the prisoners; the pain of the sick and injured; the grief of the bereaved; the frailty of the old and weak.

I am especially concerned for .... and I know you care for *them*. Give them all strength and show them your love in the way they each need it.

(Based on a prayer by St Anselm)

When Someone Has Died
Lord,
you continue to care for those who have died;
give your rest to .... that *he/she* may be with you for ever
and may enjoy the reward of everlasting life.

(Based on a prayer by St Ignatius of Loyola)

In Advent
Lord God,
we are waiting for Jesus' coming in glory;
keep me firm in our faith
that he may not find me sleeping in sin,
but busy serving him and happy praising him.

(Based on a prayer in the Gelasian sacramentary)

At Christmas

Jesus,
thank you for coming into the world.
Like your mother Mary,
I always want to be ready to obey God.
Bless all the people who do not know you,
all who ignore you, keeping Christmas just for themselves.
I have nothing to give you except my love
but I want to give as much of this as I can.
I know that when I love other people
I am also loving you –
Help me to do this.

(Abridged from a prayer by Br Kenneth CGA and
Sr Geraldine Dss CSA)

In Lent

Lord Jesus, let me come to you now:
my heart is cold; Lord, warm it with your love.
My heart is sinful; make it clean with your blood.
My heart is weak; strengthen it with the Holy Spirit.
My heart is empty; fill it with your presence.
Jesus, my heart is yours; take it and keep it for ever.

(Based on a prayer by St Augustine)

At Eastertide

Jesus,
you have shown us that the way of life leads through grief and pain,
and you have risen from the dead to new life.
Help me to choose the road you took,
and to walk with you for ever in the light of Easter.

At Pentecost

Father,
at Pentecost you gave to all races the hope of eternal life;
send your Spirit today throughout the world,
that we may proclaim and everyone hear
the Good News of your Son, Jesus Christ.

Preparing for Communion

The most important act of worship for the Church is the Eucharist, because at the Last Supper, Jesus instructed his disciples to 'Do this in remembrance of me'. So we celebrate his death and resurrection by bringing before God bread and wine, and in our communion we receive Christ's body and blood. But we should receive communion only after careful preparation; by confessing our sins; by not engaging in anything unnecessary beforehand; by deciding what or whom we are going to pray for in the Eucharist.

It is desirable to read the collect of the day beforehand, as this is the prayer that sums up all our prayers, and also the Bible readings. The pew edition of ASB contains the collects and readings for each Sunday and Holy Day, and a table of the weekday Eucharistic readings.

PREPARATION FOR HOLY COMMUNION

In the name of the Father, and of the Son, and of the Holy Spirit. Amen.

Give me grace, Lord, to see my faults and to be truly sorry.

Remember your sins and tell God you are sorry.

Have I loved God above all things, and kept my rule of life?
Have I loved my neighbour as myself ?
Have I been the sort of person God wants me to be?

A fuller self-examination is on page 11.

Father,
I have sinned against you;
I am no longer worthy to be called your child
and yet you call me to share in the Eucharist;
have mercy on me,
forgive me my sins
and strengthen my resolve to do better;
through Jesus Christ our Lord. Amen.

Decide what will be your intention at the Eucharist, what or whom you will be praying for.

Lord Jesus,
we offer this bread and this cup in your name
to the glory of your Father
and for the salvation of the whole universe;
and especially I pray for...............

Father,
the cup of blessing which we bless
is a sharing in the blood of your Son;
the bread which we break
is a sharing in his body.
Help me always to discern his presence in this holy meal
and to proclaim his death until he comes;
through Jesus Christ our Lord. Amen.

QUESTIONS FOR SELF-EXAMINATION

My Love for God

1   Is my heart set on God, so that I truly love him above everything? Or do I really think that religious matters are unimportant?

2   Am I in church every Sunday morning, whether I am serving or not? What sort of excuses do I make for not going?

3   When in church, do I take my part in the teamwork of worship seriously? Or do I let my attention wander?

4   Do I set aside each day a regular time for unhurried personal prayer? What sort of excuses do I make for speeding through my prayers or forgetting them altogether?

5   Do I make the effort to learn about the Christian faith and life and to take them seriously? Or do I think that being a Christian means no more than going to church?

6   Do I do what God wants me to do even if I want to do something different? Or am I ashamed of being a Christian and of going to church?

My Love for Other People

1   Do I truly love my family? Or do I take them for granted, expecting things to be done for me, and not taking my share in household chores?

2   Do I respect my friends and colleagues, or my boy- and girl-friends? Or do I use them for my own advantage or pleasure?

3   Have I a genuine love for all the people I meet? Or am I rude to them, impatient, jealous or quarrelsome?

4   Do I believe that giving is more important than receiving? In what sort of ways am I selfish?

5   Do I believe in and try to practise forgiveness? Or do I refuse to put things right with those who have offended me or whom I have offended?

6   Have I the right attitude towards authority and social justice? Towards other people's property or reputation?

My Love for Myself

1   Do I have a good understanding of my shortcomings and my abilities? Or do I think I am better than anybody else and refuse to listen to their point of view?

2   Do I make use of every chance I get to live life to the full, and be of as much use as I ought? Or do I bury my talents, out of false humility, cowardice or laziness?

3   Am I concerned for the truth in all things? Or do I tell lies or exaggerate, or do things I wouldn't otherwise do, simply to show off or to project a false image of myself?

4   Am I prepared to ask for advice? Or do I either bottle everything up inside or talk constantly about myself and my problems?

5   Am I faithful to the spirit of poverty and simplicity shown by Christ? Or am I too attached to belongings, my money and my spare time, too concerned to have what I want?

6   Do I take my work seriously, as something I can offer to God? Or do I approach it carelessly, lazily, or always complaining?

Finally, have I faith in God's mercy and my need for his forgiveness?

Vestry Prayers before the Eucharist

President	*In the name of the Father, and of the Son, and of the Holy Spirit.*
All	**Amen.**

President	*My help comes from the Lord*
Servers	**who has made heaven and earth.**

President	*Teach me to do your will*
Servers	**for you are my God.**

President	*O send out your light and your truth*
Servers	**and let them lead me.**

Either of the following prayers may be said:

All   **Almighty God,**
to whom all hearts are open,
all desires known,
and from whom no secrets are hidden:
cleanse the thoughts of our hearts
by the inspiration of your Holy Spirit,
that we may perfectly love you,
and worthily magnify your holy name;
through Christ our Lord. Amen.

or

President   *Father,*
your Son Jesus Christ gave his body
   to be broken on the cross;
as in this Eucharist we share his broken body
   and become united with him,
so may all your Church be brought together
   into your kingdom;
through Jesus Christ our Lord.

All   **Amen.**

President	*I shall go to the altar of God*
Servers	**to God my joy and my delight.**

The Order for Holy Communion

also called

The Eucharist

and

The Lord's Supper

Rite A

from

The Alternative Service Book 1980

The text of the Eucharist (printed in **bold** and *italic* type) on pages 15–40 follows an authorized order of The Order for Holy Communion Rite A on pages 119–173 of The Alternative Service Book 1980. Some parts of the service, for example, the Eucharistic Prayers, are not reproduced in full. Some of the rubrics have also been modified to take account of this.

Material printed on a tinted background is not part of the authorized service of Rite A, and has been included for the purpose of instruction of servers and personal prayer.

Texts in **bold** type are to be said or sung by the server and congregation.

The numbers [ASB 119], etc., indicate the corresponding pages in The Alternative Service Book 1980.

THE PREPARATION

1   At the entry of the ministers an appropriate sentence may be used;
     and a hymn, a canticle, or a psalm may be sung.

> The servers, choir and president enter in the order: crucifer and
> acolytes; choir; other servers; president. If there is a deacon or
> assistant priest, he enters the church immediately before the
> president. They all bow to the altar and take up their positions.

2   The president welcomes the people using these or other
     appropriate words.

           The Lord be with you or *The Lord is here*

All   **and also with you**   **His Spirit is with us**

or Easter Day to Pentecost

           Alleluia! Christ is risen.

All   **He is risen indeed. Alleluia!**

> 3 The Collect for Purity may be said here if it has not already been
> said in the vestry.

All   **Almighty God,**
            to whom all hearts are open,
            all desires known,
            and from whom no secrets are hidden:
            cleanse the thoughts of our hearts
            by the inspiration of your Holy Spirit,
            that we may perfectly love you,

**and worthily magnify your holy name;
through Christ our Lord. Amen.**

PRAYERS OF PENITENCE

4   The PRAYERS OF PENITENCE (sections 5–8) may be said here, or after section 23; if they are said here, sections 6–8 are always used. Alternative confessions may be used.

5   THE COMMANDMENTS (section 78, page 34) or the following SUMMARY OF THE LAW may be said.

    Minister   *Our Lord Jesus Christ said: The first commandment is this: 'Hear, O Israel, the Lord our God is the only Lord. You shall love the Lord your God with all your heart, with all your soul, with all your mind, and with all your strength.' The second is this: 'Love your neighbour as yourself.' There is no other commandment greater than these.*

    All   **Amen. Lord, have mercy.**

6   The minister invites the congregation to confess their sins in these or other suitable words (see section 25, page 31).

    God so loved the world that he gave his only Son Jesus Christ to save us from our sins, to be our advocate in heaven, and to bring us to eternal life.

    Let us confess our sins, in penitence and faith, firmly resolved to keep God's commandments and to live in love and peace with all men.

7   **All**   **Almighty God, our heavenly Father,
we have sinned against you and against our
    fellow men,
in thought and word and deed,
through negligence, through weakness,
through our own deliberate fault.
We are truly sorry,
and repent of all our sins.**

**For the sake of your Son Jesus Christ, who
    died for us,
forgive us all that is past;
and grant that we may serve you in newness
    of life
to the glory of your name. Amen.**

8   President *Almighty God,*
                who forgives all who truly repent,
                have mercy upon you,
                pardon and deliver you from all your sins,
                confirm and strengthen you in all goodness,
                and keep you in life eternal;
                through Jesus Christ our Lord. **Amen.**

9   KYRIE ELEISON may be said.

                Lord, have mercy.
                Lord, have mercy.

                Christ, have mercy.
                Christ, have mercy.

                Lord, have mercy.
                Lord, have mercy.

10   GLORIA IN EXCELSIS may be said.

     All   **Glory to God in the highest,
                and peace to his people on earth.**

                **Lord God, heavenly King,
                almighty God and Father,
                we worship you, we give you thanks,
                we praise you for your glory.**

                **Lord Jesus Christ, only Son of the Father,
                Lord God, Lamb of God,
                you take away the sin of the world:
                have mercy on us;
                you are seated at the right hand of the Father;
                receive our prayer.**

> **For you alone are the Holy One,**
> **you alone are the Lord,**
> **you alone are the Most High,**
> **Jesus Christ,**
> **with the Holy Spirit,**
> **in the glory of God the Father. Amen.**

11 The president says THE COLLECT.

THE MINISTRY OF THE WORD

12 Either two or three readings from scripture follow, the last of which is always the Gospel.

13 OLD TESTAMENT READING. At the end the reader may say

> *This is the word of the Lord.*
>
> **All**   **Thanks be to God.**

14 A PSALM may be used.

15 NEW TESTAMENT READING (EPISTLE). At the end the reader may say

> *This is the word of the Lord.*
>
> **All**   **Thanks be to God.**

> 16 During the hymn or psalm, the servers, holding their candles, go with the president or assistant to where the Gospel is to be proclaimed. One server may be required to hold the Gospel book.

17 THE GOSPEL. When it is announced

> **All**   **Glory to Christ our Saviour.**

At the end the reader says

> *This is the Gospel of Christ.*
>
> **All**   **Praise to Christ our Lord.**

> The servers lead the president or assistant and go back to their seats.

18 THE SERMON

19 THE NICENE CREED is said on Sundays and other Holy Days, and
     may be said on other days.

    All   **We believe in one God,**
                the Father, the almighty,
                maker of heaven and earth,
                of all that is,
                seen and unseen.

                We believe in one Lord, Jesus Christ,
                the only Son of God,
                eternally begotten of the Father,
                God from God, Light from Light,
                true God from true God,
                begotten, not made,
                of one Being with the Father.
                Through him all things were made.
                For us men and for our salvation
                he came down from heaven;
                by the power of the Holy Spirit
                he became incarnate of the Virgin Mary,
                    and was made man.
                For our sake he was crucified under
                    Pontius Pilate;
                he suffered death and was buried.
                On the third day he rose again
                in accordance with the Scriptures;
                he ascended into heaven
                and is seated at the right hand of the Father.
                He will come again in glory
                to judge the living and the dead,
                and his kingdom will have no end.

                We believe in the Holy Spirit,
                the Lord, the giver of life,
                who proceeds from the Father and the Son.
                With the Father and the Son he is worshipped
                    and glorified.
                He has spoken through the Prophets.

We believe in one holy catholic and
  apostolic Church.
We acknowledge one baptism for the
  forgiveness of sins.
We look for the resurrection of the dead,
and the life of the world to come. Amen.

THE INTERCESSION

20　The president or another of the congregation leads prayers for
the Church, the world, the local community, all who suffer
and the departed. The form below, or one of those in section
81 (page 37), or other suitable words, may be used.

21　This form may be used (a) with the insertion of specific subjects
between the paragraphs; (b) as a continuous whole with or without
brief biddings.

Not all paragraphs need be used on every occasion. Individual
names may be added at the places indicated. This response may be
used before or after each paragraph.

Minister　*Lord, in your mercy*
All　　　**hear our prayer.**

　　　　　*Let us pray for the Church and for the world, and let us
　　　　　thank God for his goodness.*

　　　　　*Almighty God, our heavenly Father, you promised
　　　　　through your Son Jesus Christ to hear us when we pray
　　　　　in faith.*

　　　　　*Strengthen N our bishop and all your Church in the
　　　　　service of Christ; that those who confess your name
　　　　　may be united in your truth, live together in your love,
　　　　　and reveal your glory in the world.*

　　　　　*Bless and guide Elizabeth our Queen; give wisdom to
　　　　　all in authority; and direct this and every nation in the
　　　　　ways of justice and of peace; that men may honour one
　　　　　another, and seek the common good.*

Give grace to us, our families and friends, and to all our neighbours; that we may serve Christ in one another, and love as he loves us.

Comfort and heal all those who suffer in body, mind, or spirit...; give them courage and hope in their troubles; and bring them the joy of your salvation.

Hear us as we remember those who have died in the faith of Christ...; according to your promises, grant us with them a share in your eternal kingdom.

Rejoicing in the fellowship of (N and of) all your saints, we commend ourselves and all Christian people to your unfailing love.

	Merciful Father,
All	**accept these prayers**
	for the sake of your Son,
	our Saviour Jesus Christ. Amen.

PRAYERS OF PENITENCE

23–28 The PRAYERS OF PENITENCE are said here, if they have not been said previously (see sections 4–8).

29 All may say

> **We do not presume**
> **to come to this your table, merciful Lord,**
> **trusting in our own righteousness,**
> **but in your manifold and great mercies.**
> **We are not worthy**
> **so much as to gather up the crumbs under**
> **   your table.**
> **But you are the same Lord**
> **whose nature is always to have mercy.**
> **Grant us therefore, gracious Lord,**
> **so to eat the flesh of your dear son,**
> **   Jesus Christ**
> **and to drink his blood,**
> **that we may evermore dwell in him**
> **and he in us. Amen.**

The alternative prayer at section 82 (page 40) may be used.

THE MINISTRY OF THE SACRAMENT

THE PEACE

30   The president says either of the following or other suitable words
(see section 83).

> *Christ is our peace.*
> *He has reconciled us to God*
>   *in one body by the cross.*
> *We meet in his name and share his peace.*

or
> *We are the Body of Christ.*
> *In the one Spirit we were all baptized into*
>   *one body.*
> *Let us then pursue all that makes for peace*
> *and builds up our common life.*

83   **A SELECTION OF OTHER INTRODUCTORY WORDS TO
THE PEACE**

Advent, Christmas, Epiphany
> Our Saviour Christ is the Prince of Peace; of the
> increase of his government and of peace there shall
> be no end.

Lent
> Being justified by faith, we have peace with God
> through our Lord Jesus Christ.

Easter, Ascension
> The risen Christ came and stood among his disciples
> and said, Peace be with you. Then they were glad
> when they saw the Lord.

Pentecost
> The fruit of the Spirit is love, joy, peace. If we live in
> the Spirit, let us walk in the Spirit.

Saints' Days
> We are fellow-citizens with the saints, and of the
> household of God, through Christ our Lord who
> came and preached peace to those who were far off
> and those who were near.

The president then says

> *The peace of the Lord be always with you*
>
> **All** **and also with you.**

31 The president may say

> *Let us offer one another a sign of peace.*

and all may exchange a sign of peace.

THE PREPARATION OF THE GIFTS

> The servers may bring the chalices from the credence table to the altar. Then they receive from the representatives of the congregation the ciborium containing the wafers of bread and the cruets containing water and wine. The first server hands the ciborium to the president, who praises God, saying
>
> > *Blessed are you, Lord, God of all creation.*
> > *Through your goodness we have this bread to offer,*
> > *which earth has given and human hands have*
> > *made. It will become for us the bread of life.*

> **All** **Blessed be God for ever.**

> The second server meanwhile has removed the stoppers of the cruets, and presents them to the president, the wine in the right hand and the water in the left. When the president has taken the wine, the server transfers the water cruet into the right hand and accepts the wine cruet in his or her left. When the president has filled the chalices with wine and water, the server replaces the cruets on the credence table. The president praises God over the wine, saying
>
> > *Blessed are you, Lord, God of all creation.*
> > *Through your goodness we have this wine to offer,*
> > *fruit of the vine and work of human hands.*
> > *It will become our spiritual drink.*

> **All** **Blessed be God for ever.**

> A hymn is usually sung while the collection is taken; one of the servers receives the collection from the sidesmen and gives it to the president.

34 All may say

> Yours, Lord, is the greatness, the power,
> the glory, the splendour, and the majesty;
> for everything in heaven and on earth is yours.
> All things come from you,
> and of your own do we give you.

Then the president returns the collection to the server.

Finally, one of the servers pours water over the president's fingers into the lavabo bowl, and the president dries them with the towel placed over the server's left wrist.

THE EUCHARISTIC PRAYER
THE TAKING OF THE BREAD AND CUP AND
THE GIVING OF THANKS

36 The president takes the bread and cup into his hands and replaces them on the holy table.

While the president says one of the four Eucharistic Prayers, the two servers hold their candles high. In the Eucharistic Prayer, the president on behalf of the whole congregation gives thanks for the mighty acts of God, and especially for the incarnation of Jesus Christ. We commemorate his death and resurrection by repeating what he did at the Last Supper, by taking bread and wine, and we pray that they will be accepted by God and become Christ's Body and Blood. This is the climax of the service, and in some churches a bell or gong is rung to mark the consecration of the bread and wine.

38/39/40/41   Each prayer begins

President *The Lord be with you*   or   *The Lord is here.*
All   **and also with you.**   **His Spirit is with us.**

President *Lift up your hearts.*
All   **We lift them to the Lord.**

President *Let us give thanks to the Lord our God.*
All   **It is right to give him thanks and praise.**

> After the preface, the first part of the Eucharistic Prayer, the people all say or sing

> Holy, holy, holy Lord,
> God of power and might,
> heaven and earth are full of your glory.
> Hosanna in the highest.
>
> Blessed is he who comes in the name of the Lord.
> Hosanna in the highest.

> After the words of institution, the words that Jesus spoke to his disciples at the Last Supper, the people are invited to proclaim the mystery of faith.

All   **Christ has died:**
             Christ is risen:
             Christ will come again.

> The prayer is said by the president alone, but it is the prayer of the whole people of God; therefore everyone must make the prayer his own by saying **Amen** at the end. If the First Eucharistic Prayer is used, the people join with the president saying

> **Blessing and honour and glory and power**
> **be yours for ever and ever. Amen.**

THE COMMUNION
THE BREAKING OF THE BREAD AND
THE GIVING OF THE BREAD AND CUP

42   THE LORD'S PRAYER is said either as follows or in its traditional form.

President *As our Saviour taught us, so we pray.*
All   **Our Father in heaven,**
             hallowed be your name,
             your kingdom come,

your will be done,
on earth as in heaven.
Give us today our daily bread.
Forgive us our sins
as we forgive those who sin against us.
Lead us not into temptation
but deliver us from evil.

For the kingdom, the power, and the glory are
   yours
now and for ever. Amen.

43   The president breaks the consecrated bread, saying

We break this bread
to share in the body of Christ.
All   **Though we are many, we are one body,**
because we all share in one bread.

44   Either here or during the distribution one of the following
ANTHEMS may be said.

All   **Lamb of God, you take away the sins of**
the world:
have mercy on us.

Lamb of God, you take away the sins of
the world:
have mercy on us.

Lamb of God, you take away the sins of
the world:
grant us peace.

or   **Jesus, Lamb of God: have mercy on us.**
Jesus, bearer of our sins: have mercy on us.
Jesus, redeemer of the world: give us your
peace.

45   Before the distribution the president says

Draw near with faith. Receive the body of our Lord Jesus

Christ which he gave for you, and his blood which he shed for you.

Eat and drink in remembrance that he died for you, and feed on him in your hearts by faith with thanksgiving.

85 He may also say

Jesus is the Lamb of God
who takes away the sins of the world.
Happy are those who are called to his supper.

All **Lord, I am not worthy to receive you,**
but only say the word, and I shall be healed.

or

President The gifts of God for the people of God.

All **Jesus Christ is holy,**
Jesus Christ is Lord,
to the glory of God the Father.

or from Easter Day to Pentecost

President Alleluia! Christ our Passover is sacrificed for us.

All **Alleluia! Let us keep the feast.**

46 The president and people receive the communion. At the distribution the minister says to each communicant

The body of Christ keep you in eternal life.
The blood of Christ keep you in eternal life.

or The body of Christ.
The blood of Christ.

The communicant replies each time **Amen**, and then receives.

Alternative words of distribution may be found in section 66 (page 32).

47 During the distribution hymns and anthems may be sung.

48 If either or both of the consecrated elements be likely to prove insufficient, the president himself returns to the holy table and adds more, saying these words.

> *Father, giving thanks over the bread and the cup according to the institution of your Son Jesus Christ, who said, Take, eat; this is my body (and/or Drink this; this is my blood), we pray that this bread/wine also may be to us his body/blood, to be received in remembrance of him.*

49 Any consecrated bread and wine which is not required for purposes of communion is consumed at the end of the distribution or after the service.

AFTER COMMUNION

50 An appropriate sentence may be said and a hymn may be sung.

51 Either or both of the following prayers or other suitable prayers are said.

52 President *Father of all, we give you thanks and praise, that when we were still far off you met us in your Son and brought us home. Dying and living, he declared your love, gave us grace, and opened the gate of glory. May we who share Christ's body live his risen life; we who drink his cup bring life to others; we whom the Spirit lights give*

light to the world. Keep us firm in the hope you have set before us, so we and all your children shall be free, and the whole earth live to praise your name; through Christ our Lord. **Amen.**

or

53 **All**   **Almighty God,**
we thank you for feeding us
with the body and blood of your Son Jesus Christ.
Through him we offer you our souls and bodies
to be a living sacrifice.
Send us out
in the power of your Spirit
to live and work
to your praise and glory. Amen.

THE DISMISSAL

54 The president may say this or an alternative BLESSING (section 77, page 32).

The peace of God, which passes all understanding, keep your hearts and minds in the knowledge and love of God, and of his Son Jesus Christ our Lord; and the blessing of God almighty, the Father, the Son, and the Holy Spirit, be among you, and remain with you always. **Amen.**

55 *President* *Go in peace to love and serve the Lord.*
All   **In the name of Christ. Amen.**

or

President *Go in the peace of Christ.*
All   **Thanks be to God.**

From Easter Day to Pentecost 'Alleluia! Alleluia!' may be added after both the versicle and the response.

56 The ministers and people depart.

The crucifer and acolytes bow to the altar and lead the choir and president to the vestry. In the vestry the president may say

The Lord be with you
All   **and also with you.**

President Let us bless the Lord.
All   Thanks be to God.

President May the divine assistance remain with us always.

THANKS AFTER COMMUNION

After making communion or at the end of the Eucharist, give thanks to God for the gift of Christ's body and blood. These prayers may help.

Father,
in this sacrament of the body and blood of Jesus
we share in his suffering and his death;
help us to love one another
as he loved us and laid down his life for his friends,
that we may share in his resurrection;
through Jesus Christ our Lord.

Christ Jesus,
  in Holy Communion I find you
  under the forms of bread and wine;
  in my everyday life I find you
  in all the people I meet,
  especially when they need help.
For you said,
  Anything you do for one of my brothers
  You do for me.

(Mother Teresa of Calcutta)

Father,
I was hungry, and in the Eucharist you give me food,
I was thirsty, and you give me drink;
teach me to follow you with willing heart in every
    sphere of life;
through Jesus Christ our Lord.

Jesus Lord Christ,
   You lived for us;
   You died for us.
Make me like you.
   Save me;
   Free me from sin;
   Give me your strength.
Good Jesus,
   Don't let me be separated from you,
   Defend me from evil
   And one day call me to you
   That with your other friends
   I may praise you for ever.

(Based on the Anima Christi)

APPENDICES

25 ALTERNATIVE INVITATION TO CONFESSION

The minister may say one or more of these SENTENCES instead of the first paragraph at section 6.

Hear the words of comfort our Saviour Christ says to all who truly turn to him: Come to me, all who labour and are heavy laden, and I will give you rest.   Matt. 11: 28

God so loved the world that he gave his only Son, that whoever believes in him should not perish but have eternal life.   John 3: 16

Hear what Saint Paul says: This saying is true and worthy of full acceptance, that Christ Jesus came into the world to save sinners.   1 Timothy 1: 15

Hear what Saint John says: If anyone sins, we have an advocate with the Father, Jesus Christ the righteous; and he is the propitiation for our sins.   1 John 2: 1

66 ALTERNATIVE WORDS OF DISTRIBUTION

Minister   *The body of our Lord Jesus Christ, which was given for you, preserve your body and soul to eternal life. Take and eat this in remembrance that Christ died for you, and feed on him in your heart by faith with thanksgiving.*

The blood of our Lord Jesus Christ, which was shed for you, preserve your body and soul to eternal life. Drink this in remembrance that Christ's blood was shed for you, and be thankful.

77 ALTERNATIVE BLESSINGS

Advent

Christ the Sun of Righteousness shine upon you and scatter the darkness from before your path; and the blessing...

Christmas

Christ, who by his incarnation gathered into one all things earthly and heavenly, fill you with his joy and peace; and the blessing...

or

Christ the Son of God, born of Mary, fill you with his grace to trust his promises and obey his will; and the blessing...

Epiphany

Christ the Son of God gladden your hearts with the good news of his kingdom; and the blessing...

Ash Wednesday to Lent 4

Christ give you grace to grow in holiness, to deny yourselves, take up your cross, and follow him; and the blessing...

Lent 5 and Holy Week

Christ crucified draw you to himself, to find in him a sure ground for faith, a firm support for hope, and the assurance of sins forgiven; and the blessing...

Easter

The God of peace, who brought again from the dead our Lord Jesus, that great shepherd of the sheep, through the blood of the eternal covenant, make you perfect in every good work to do his will, working in you that which is well-pleasing in his sight; and the blessing...

[ASB 150/59]

or

The God of peace, who brought again from the dead our Lord Jesus, that great shepherd of the sheep, make you perfect in every good work to do his will; and the blessing...

or

God the Father, by whose glory Christ was raised from the dead, strengthen you to walk with him in his risen life; and the blessing...

or

God, who through the resurrection of our Lord Jesus Christ has given us the victory, give you joy and peace in your faith; and the blessing...

Ascension
Christ our king make you faithful and strong to do his will, that you may reign with him in glory; and the blessing...

Pentecost
The Spirit of truth lead you into all truth, give you grace to confess that Jesus Christ is Lord, and to proclaim the word and works of God; and the blessing...

Trinity Sunday
God the Holy Trinity make you strong in faith and love, defend you on every side, and guide you in truth and peace; and the blessing...

Saints' Days
God give you grace to follow his saints in faith and hope and love; and the blessing...

or

God give you grace to follow his saints in faith and truth and gentleness; and the blessing...

or

God give you grace to share the inheritance of his saints in glory; and the blessing...

Unity
Christ the Good Shepherd, who laid down his life for the sheep, draw you and all who hear his voice to be one within one fold; and the blessing...

General
The God of all grace who called you to his eternal glory in Christ Jesus, establish, strengthen and settle you in the faith; and the blessing...

or

God, who from the death of sin raised you to new life in Christ, keep you from falling and set you in the presence of his glory; and the blessing...

or

Christ who has nourished us with himself the living bread, make you one in praise and love, and raise you up at the last day; and the blessing...

or

The God of peace fill you with all joy and hope in believing; and the blessing...

78 THE COMMANDMENTS
Either A:

Minister   *Our Lord Jesus Christ said, If you love me, keep my commandments; happy are those who hear the word of God and keep it. Hear then these commandments which God has given to his people, and take them to heart.*

                I am the Lord your God: you shall have no other gods but me.
                You shall love the Lord your God with all your heart, with all your soul, with all your mind and with all your strength.

All   **Amen, Lord, have mercy.**

Minister   *You shall not make for yourself any idol.*
                God is spirit, and those who worship him must worship in spirit and in truth.

All   **Amen. Lord, have mercy.**

Minister   *You shall not dishonour the name of the Lord your God. You shall worship him with awe and reverence.*

All	**Amen. Lord, have mercy.**

Minister	Remember the Lord's day and keep it holy. Christ is risen from the dead: set your minds on things that are above, not on things that are on the earth.
All	**Amen. Lord, have mercy.**

Minister	Honour your father and mother. Live as servants of God; honour all men; love the brotherhood.
All	**Amen. Lord, have mercy.**

Minister	You shall not commit murder. Be reconciled to your brother; overcome evil with good.
All	**Amen. Lord, have mercy.**

Minister	You shall not commit adultery. Know that your body is a temple of the Holy Spirit.
All	**Amen. Lord, have mercy.**

Minister	You shall not steal. Be honest in all that you do and care for those in need.
All	**Amen. Lord, have mercy.**

Minister	You shall not be a false witness. Let everyone speak the truth.
All	**Amen. Lord, have mercy.**

Minister	You shall not covet anything which belongs to your neighbour. Remember the words of the Lord Jesus: It is more blessed to give than to receive. Love your neighbour as yourself, for love is the fulfilling of the law.
All	**Amen. Lord, have mercy.**

or B:

Minister	God spoke all these words, saying, I am the Lord your God (who brought you out of the land of Egypt, out of the house of bondage). You shall have no other gods before me.
All	**Amen. Lord, have mercy.**

Minister You shall not make for yourself a graven image (or any likeness of anything that is in heaven above, or that is in the earth beneath, or that is in the water under the earth; you shall not bow down to them or serve them; for I the Lord your God am a jealous God, visiting the iniquity of the fathers upon the children to the third and the fourth generation of those who hate me, but showing steadfast love to thousands of those who love me and keep my commandments).

All **Amen. Lord, have mercy.**

Minister You shall not take the name of the Lord your God in vain (for the Lord will not hold him guiltless who takes his name in vain).

All **Amen. Lord, have mercy.**

Minister Remember the sabbath day, to keep it holy. (Six days you shall labour, and do all your work; but the seventh day is a sabbath to the Lord your God; in it you shall not do any work, you, or your son, or your daughter, your manservant, or your maidservant, or your cattle, or the sojourner who is within your gates; for in six days the Lord made heaven and earth, the sea, and all that is in them, and rested the seventh day; therefore the Lord blessed the sabbath day and hallowed it.)

All **Amen. Lord, have mercy.**

Minister Honour your father and your mother (that your days may be long in the land which the Lord your God gives you).

All **Amen. Lord, have mercy.**

Minister You shall not kill.
All **Amen. Lord, have mercy.**

Minister You shall not commit adultery.
All **Amen. Lord, have mercy.**

Minister You shall not steal.
All **Amen. Lord, have mercy.**

Minister You shall not bear false witness against your neighbour.

[ASB 163-64]

All	**Amen. Lord, have mercy.**
Minister	*You shall not covet (your neighbour's house; you shall not covet your neighbour's wife, or his manservant, or his maidservant, or his ox, or his ass, or) anything that is your neighbour's.*
All	**Lord, have mercy, and write all these your laws in our hearts.**

81 **ALTERNATIVE FORMS OF INTERCESSION**
Either A:

Minister	*Let us pray for the whole Church of God in Christ Jesus, and for all men according to their needs.*
	O God, the creator and preserver of all mankind, we pray for men of every race, and in every kind of need: make your ways known on earth, your saving power among the nations. (Especially we pray for...) *Lord, in your mercy*
All	**hear our prayer.**

Minister	*We pray for your Church throughout the world: guide and govern us by your Holy Spirit, that all who profess and call themselves Christians may be led into the way of truth, and hold the faith in unity of spirit, in the bond of peace, and in righteousness of life. (Especially we pray for...)* *Lord, in your mercy*
All	**hear our prayer.**

Minister	*We commend to your fatherly goodness all who are anxious or distressed in mind or body; comfort and relieve them in their need; give them patience in their sufferings, and bring good out of their troubles. (Especially we pray for...)* *Merciful Father,*
All	**accept these prayers** **for the sake of your Son,** **our Saviour Jesus Christ. Amen.**

or B:

Minister   *In the power of the Spirit and in union with Christ, let us pray to the Father.*

Hear our prayers, O Lord our God.
All   **Hear us, good Lord.**

Minister   *Govern and direct your holy Church; fill it with love and truth; and grant it that unity which is your will.*
All   **Hear us, good Lord.**

Minister   *Give us boldness to preach the gospel in all the world, and to make disciples of all the nations.*
All   **Hear us, good Lord.**

Minister   *Enlighten your ministers with knowledge and understanding, that by their teaching and their lives they may proclaim your word.*
All   **Hear us, good Lord.**

Minister   *Give your people grace to hear and receive your word, and to bring forth the fruit of the Spirit.*
All   **Hear us, good Lord.**

Minister   *Bring into the way of truth all who have erred and are deceived.*
All   **Hear us, good Lord.**

Minister   *Strengthen those who stand; comfort and help the faint-hearted; raise up the fallen; and finally beat down Satan under our feet.*
All   **Hear us, good Lord.**

Minister   *Guide the leaders of the nations into the ways of peace and justice.*
All   **Hear us, good Lord.**

Minister   *Guard and strengthen your servant Elizabeth our Queen, that she may put her trust in you, and seek your honour and glory.*
All   **Hear us, good Lord.**

Minister   *Endue the High Court of Parliament and all the Ministers of the Crown with wisdom and understanding.*

All   **Hear us, good Lord.**

Minister   *Bless those who administer the law, that they may uphold justice, honesty, and truth.*
All   **Hear us, good Lord.**

Minister   *Teach us to use the fruits of the earth to your glory, and for the good of all mankind.*
All   **Hear us, good Lord.**

Minister   *Bless and keep your people.*
All   **Hear us, good Lord.**

Minister   *Help and comfort the lonely, the bereaved, and the oppressed.*
All   **Lord, have mercy.**

Minister   *Keep in safety those who travel, and all who are in danger.*
All   **Lord, have mercy.**

Minister   *Heal the sick in body and mind, and provide for the homeless, the hungry, and the destitute.*
All   **Lord, have mercy.**

Minister   *Show your pity on prisoners and refugees, and all who are in trouble.*
All   **Lord, have mercy.**

Minister   *Forgive our enemies, persecutors, and slanderers, and turn their hearts.*
All   **Lord, have mercy.**

Minister   *Hear us as we remember those who have died in the peace of Christ, both those who have confessed the faith and those whose faith in known to you alone, and grant us with them a share in your eternal kingdom.*
All   **Lord, have mercy.**

Minister   *Father, you hear those who pray in the name of your Son: grant that what we have asked in faith we may obtain according to your will; through Jesus Christ our Lord. Amen.*

82 **ALTERNATIVE PRAYER OF HUMBLE ACCESS (section 29)**

> Most merciful Lord,
> your love compels us to come in.
> Our hands were unclean,
> our hearts were unprepared;
> we were not fit
> even to eat the crumbs from under your table.
> But you, Lord, are the God of our salvation,
> and share your bread with sinners.
> So cleanse and feed us
> with the precious body and blood of your Son,
> that he may live in us and we in him;
> and that we, with the whole company of Christ,
> may sit and eat in your kingdom. Amen.

NOTES

1 *Preparation*   Careful devotional preparation before the service is recommended for every communicant.

2 *The President*   The president (who, in accordance with the provisions of Canon B12 'Of the ministry of the Holy Communion', must have been episcopally ordained priest) presides over the whole service. He says the opening Greeting, the Collect, the Absolution, the Peace, and the Blessing; he himself must take the bread and the cup before replacing them on the holy table, say the Eucharistic Prayer, break the consecrated bread, and receive the sacrament on every occasion. The remaining parts of the service he may delegate to others. When necessity dictates, a deacon or lay person may preside over the Ministry of the Word.

When the Bishop is present, it is appropriate that he should act as president. He may also delegate sections 32–49 to a priest.

3 *Posture*   The Eucharistic Prayer (sections 38, 39, 40, and 41) is a single prayer, the unity of which may be obscured by changes of posture in the course of it.

4 *Seasonal Material* The seasonal sentences and blessings are optional. Any other appropriate scriptural sentences may be read at sections 1 and 50 at the discretion of the president and 'Alleluia' may be added to any sentence from Easter Day until Pentecost.

5 *Greetings (section 2, etc.)* In addition to the points where greetings are provided, at other suitable points (e.g. before the Gospel and before the Blessing and Dismissal) the minister may say 'The Lord be with you' and the congregation reply 'and also with you'.

6 *Prayers of Penitence* These are used either after section 4 or section 23.

7 *Kyrie eleison (section 9)* This may be used in English or Greek.

8 *Gloria in excelsis (section 10)* This canticle may be appropriately omitted during Advent and Lent, and on weekdays which are not Principal or Greater Holy Days. It may also be used at section 1 and before section 17.

9 *The Collect (section 11)* The Collect may be introduced by the words 'Let us pray' and a brief bidding, after which silence may be kept.

10 *Readings* Where one of the three readings is to be omitted, provision for this is found in Table 3 of the Alternative Calendar and Lectionary according to the season of the year.

11 *The Gospel in Holy Week (section 17)* From Palm Sunday to the Wednesday in Holy Week, and on Good Friday, the Passion Gospel may be introduced: 'The Passion of our Lord Jesus Christ according to N', and concluded: 'This is the Passion of the Lord'. No responses are used.

12 *The Sermon (section 18)* The sermon is an integral part of the Ministry of the Word. A sermon should normally be preached at all celebrations on Sundays and other Holy Days.

15 *Acclamations* These are optional. They may be introduced by the president with the words 'Let us proclaim the mystery of faith' or with other suitable words or they may be used without introduction.

16   *Manual Acts*   In addition to the taking of the bread and the cup before the Eucharistic Prayer the president may use traditional manual acts during the Eucharistic Prayers.

17   *Words of Invitation (section 45)*   The words provided are to be used at least on Sundays and other Holy Days, and those in section 85 (page 27) may be added. On other days those in section 85 may be substituted.

18   *The Blessing (section 54)*   In addition to the blessings provided here and on pages 32–34 the president may at his discretion use others.

19   *Notices*   Banns of marriage and other notices may be published after section 2, section 19 or section 53.

20   *Hymns, Canticles, the Peace, the Collection and Presentation of the Offerings of the People, and the Preparation of the Gifts of Bread and Wine*   Points are indicated for these, but if occasion requires they may occur elsewhere.

21   *Silence*   After sections 6, 13, 15, 17, 18, before sections 42 and 51, and after the biddings in section 21, silence may be kept.

PART 2

On Serving

In the Eucharist we all have our part to play, as president, as a chorister or a sidesman, as a reader or simply an ordinary lay person. But the server, assisting the president at the altar, is far more conspicuous, and therefore should always be unostentatious, attentive and well-behaved, not just as a sign of respect to God but also as an example to others in the church. This means that the only time the server will be noticed is when he or she is inattentive or badly behaved, when he or she is causing a distraction and preventing God's people from concentrating on the celebration of the Eucharist. It is all too easy to serve badly, either by being careless and untidy, or by showing off in one's devotion. To serve well demands that certain principles must be remembered:

1 When walking in procession or in the sanctuary, always move slowly and reverently; never step backwards or sideways; do not cut corners.

2 Whenever passing the altar, stop and bow, except when the Blessed Sacrament is on it, when you should bow deeply or genuflect. When genuflecting, remember to go down on your right knee keeping your back and head straight.

    If the Sacrament is reserved on the altar, genuflect also at the beginning of the Eucharist when arriving in the sanctuary, and at the end when leaving.

3 Unless holding something, always keep your hands joined; if carrying a candle in procession, place your outer hand above your inner hand on the candlestick.

4 When standing, remain still and do not shuffle; fix your attention on what is happening in the Eucharist and join in the congregational parts. After you have made your communion, say your own prayers or sing the hymn, rather than watch the people at the rail.

5 If you do make a mistake, do not draw attention to it and cause a greater distraction!

6   Always make every effort to arrive in good time before the Eucharist begins; all the preparations must be made and the candles lit. When lighting the candles on the altar, remember that those on the south side, the right when facing the altar, are always lit first, starting from the centre. You may be called upon to check that the hymn boards are correct and in place, or to assist the sacristan in laying out the vestments and preparing the credence table. After the Eucharist, it is your job to snuff out the candles and to help clear the sanctuary.

Sanctuary and Sacristy

THE SANCTUARY

The **altar** is the most important piece of furniture in the church, as it is the table at which the Eucharist is celebrated, a symbol of Christ in the midst of his Church, and a reminder of his unrepeatable sacrifice on the cross. As a result the altar is normally the focal point of every church building, the place towards which all the architecture directs our eyes. Churches are built in all shapes and sizes, from majestic cathedrals to ancient village churches, from Victorian gothic structures to modern multi-purpose buildings; and yet almost without exception, when we look inside, it is an altar that demands our attention, because the church building exists primarily as a place where the Church can obey the command of its founder by celebrating the Eucharist. But because styles of our churches vary so much, it is not surprising that the appearance of the altar should differ from church to church.

In one building, the altar may be found against the east wall and raised on a number of steps, with a **reredos** of elaborate carving or painting on the wall above. Hanging from the front of the altar is a heavy curtain in the colour of the season, known as the **frontal**. There are six **candles** on a shelf behind the altar, and in the middle of the altar itself, a **tabernacle** containing the Blessed Sacrament for the communion of the sick; to show this a white light burns in a lamp suspended from the roof. On the altar steps stands a bell, which is rung during the Eucharistic Prayer to announce the consecration of the bread and wine.

In another church, the altar may also be against the east wall but with a wooden framework around it, from which hang curtains on three sides. The curtain at the back is known as the **dorsal** and those at the side as the **riddels**; the uprights of the framework – the riddel posts – are surmounted with gilded carved angels, or perhaps candles. There are two candles on the altar as a sign of Christ who is the Light of the World, but the Blessed Sacrament is reserved in a side chapel, in an **aumbry**, a small safe let into the north wall.

In a third church, the altar may always be called the **Holy Table**. Made of wood, it stands against the east wall, but no curtains or candles decorate it. Instead bowls of flowers have been placed on it and a brass book-stand holding the prayer book open ready for the service.

In a fourth church, the altar may be away from the wall so that the priest can stand behind it to preside at the Eucharist. Over it stands a high canopy, called a **ciborium**, **tester** or **baldacchino**. There are two candles, and between them on the altar, either a **crucifix** or a plain **cross**, the first signifying Christ's redeeming death, the other his mighty resurrection and glorious ascension. Above, hanging from the ciborium is a **pyx**, which, like the aumbry and tabernacle, holds the Blessed Sacrament.

Lastly, the altar in our fifth church may be built of local stone to a modern design and stands in the middle of the church. There are candles at each end and the **processional cross** is kept behind it. A reading-desk stands close by and a stool, for the president to use during the Ministry of the Word.

Few churches will be exactly like any of these examples, as each church is different and the layout of its furniture will differ too; but the server should be familiar with the names of the fittings and utensils of the sanctuary and with their use and symbolism. The servers usually light the candles before the service and snuff them out afterwards. They may also be called upon to set on the **credence table** the bread box, wine and water cruets and lavabo, or to replace, at the end of the service, the **altar cover** over the **fair linen**, the white cloth that is spread on the top of the altar.

In churches which use **incense**, which as it burns symbolizes the prayers of God's people rising to heaven, servers should understand the job of the **thurifer**, who carries the burning incense. As Denis Taylor comments, 'There is much prejudice against incense as a Roman custom, but its use has always been much wider than any one Christian communion.'

THE SACRED VESSELS

Before the Eucharist, the vessels that are to be used must be made ready; usually the priest or the sacristan will do this, but a server may be asked to help. The **chalice** is the name given to the ornate cup used to hold the Precious Blood of Christ, the consecrated wine of the Eucharist; the **paten** is the circular plate that holds the bread, and it usually has a shallow depression slightly smaller than the rim of the chalice. The **ciborium** is the name given to the covered bowl that holds the wafers of bread when there are to be many communicants.

To prepare the chalice, first of all place over it the **purificator** – the folded rectangle of cloth used to cleanse it after communion – then place the paten, holding a priest's wafer, over the purificator. The **pall**, which is used to prevent dust falling into the chalice, rests on top again. Then the chalice is covered with the **veil**, and a **burse**, containing the **corporal**, the cloth on which the chalice will stand on the altar, is placed on top. Sometimes a paten will not be used, and the priest's wafer will be put in the ciborium with the small wafers.

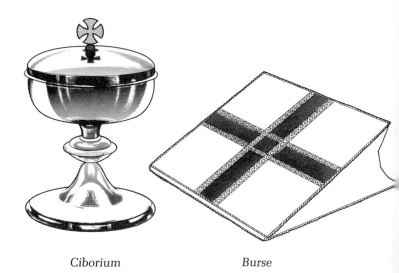

Ciborium   Burse

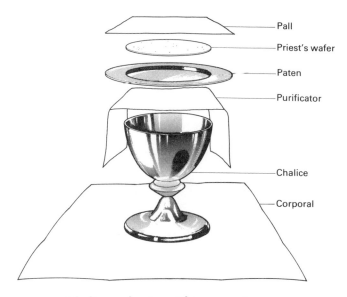

Pall

Priest's wafer

Paten

Purificator

Chalice

Corporal

Chalice and paten with ornamenta

THE VESTMENTS

The clothes we wear are very important; it would be rude to go to a smart dinner party in tee-shirt and jeans, and it would be very foolish to do a dirty job in one's best clothes. Of course God does not mind what we wear to church because it is the preparation we have made that is far more important; but our spiritual preparation should be matched by the care we give to our personal appearance.

Because the priest has the special role of presiding at the Eucharist, he has special clothes to wear, clothes which show he helps to focus the prayers of all the people on the action of the Eucharist. Servers are not quasi-priestly figures and need not wear a special costume; but because they are easily visible it may help if they are wearing a simple uniform so as not to distract the rest of the congregation. Whatever they wear, it is helpful for servers to know the names of the important vestments, and how to lay them out before the Eucharist for the priest to vest easily.

Cassock

Choir Dress
The **cassock** is the everyday wear of the clergy, and in church their undergarment; it is also often worn by choir and servers.

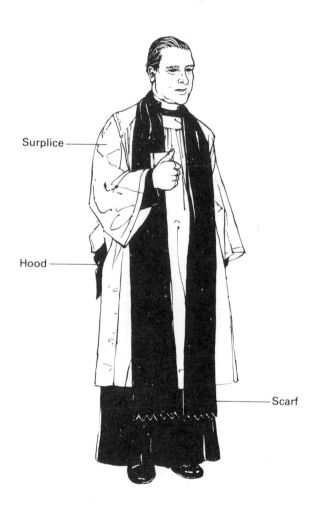

Surplice

Hood

Scarf

The **surplice** is a full white shift worn by clergy and others in choir, and sometimes by servers; clergy often wear a **scarf** and academic **hood** over the surplice, or a **stole**.

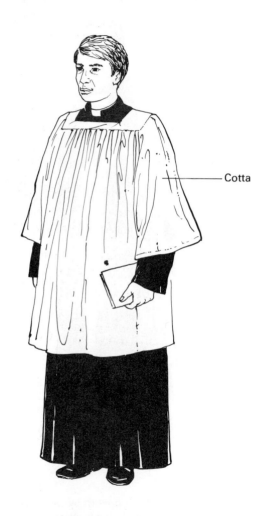

Cotta

The **cotta** is a shorter version of the surplice.

———— Amice

Eucharistic Vestments

The **amice** is a rectangular piece of white linen, tied round the shoulders of the wearer; sometimes the amice has an apparel, that is, a stiff decorated collar.

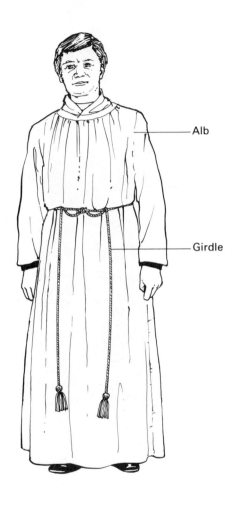

Alb

Girdle

The **alb** is a long white garment that covers the whole body; it is worn by the ministers at the Eucharist and often by servers. The **girdle** is a white cord used to secure the alb at the waist; many modern albs do not require a girdle or an amice.

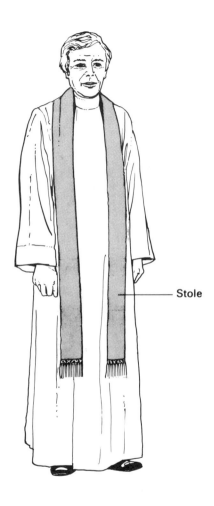

Stole

The **stole** is a strip of coloured material worn as the badge of Holy Order. A deacon wears it over one shoulder and tied at the hip; a priest or bishop wears it over both shoulders. Its colour depends on the season of the Church's year (see pages 57–59).

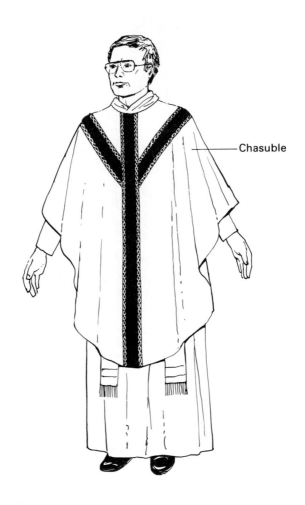

Chasuble

The **chasuble** is the priest's outer garment at the Eucharist, and is the colour of the season to match the stole.

Dalmatic

The **dalmatic** is the outer garment correctly worn by a deacon and matches the president's stole and chasuble. The **tunicle** is the outer garment of the subdeacon at a solemn Eucharist; it is similar to a dalmatic and sometimes worn by the crucifer.

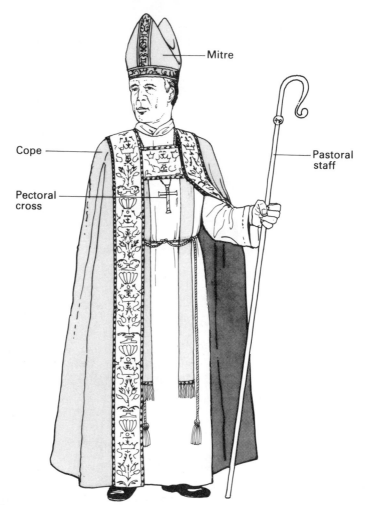

Mitre

Cope

Pastoral
staff

Pectoral
cross

Other Vestments
The **cope** is an ornate cloak, opening at the front and worn for
processions. The **mitre** is the head-dress of a bishop, who will also wear
a **pectoral cross** and may carry a **pastoral staff**.

Laying out Vestments for the Eucharist

The vestments should be laid out on a vesting chest or table in order, so that the president can put them on without trouble or confusion. The chasuble is put on last so should be laid flat on the chest first of all with the back upwards and folded over. Then the stole and the girdle are placed on the chasuble. There was a custom that stole, maniple and girdle should be laid to form the sacred monogram IHS. Now that the maniple is no longer worn, this custom cannot be followed, and it is suggested that the stole is laid in the form of an alpha (**A**) and the girdle an omega (Ω). The alb is then folded and placed over the vestments so that it can be put on easily, and the amice laid as a cover to everything else, with the tapes folded inwards.

The Church's Year

THE CHRISTMAS CYCLE

The colour of the vestments and of the burse and veil depends on the season of the Church's year or the Holy Day that is being observed; the altar frontal and the pulpit fall are also changed according to the Church season. In ASB, the Church's year starts with the ninth Sunday before Christmas, when the themes of the readings remind us of God's work told in the Old Testament; the colour is green. The fourth Sunday before Christmas is **Advent Sunday**, when the colour changes to violet, the colour of repentance, and we consider God's preparation for the birth of his son.

At **Christmas** the vestments and hangings are white; there may be a Midnight Mass with a procession around the church, when the crib is blessed. Twelve days after Christmas comes **Epiphany**, when the Church remembers the visit of the wise men to the Christ child, and the revelation of God's son to the world. The liturgical colour for Epiphany and the Sunday after is white, but then it is replaced by green, the colour of nature. In the period after Epiphany, the feast of the Presentation of our Lord falls on 2 February; this is sometimes called **Candlemas**, and lighted candles are carried in procession before the Eucharist to remind us that Christ is 'a light to reveal God to the nations'. On this day, the altar should be vested in white.

LENT

Ash Wednesday marks the beginning of Lent, when the colour of the vestments is violet again. In some churches, a Lenten Array is used instead, with vestments and frontal of unbleached linen. On Ash Wednesday the palm crosses from last year's Palm Sunday may be burnt, and in the Eucharist, after the Gospel (or sermon if there is one), the people are marked with a cross on their foreheads using the ashes, as a sign of repentance. Lent is a time of penitence and preparation for Easter; during Lent we are encouraged to practise some form of self-denial, by giving up some luxury, and to save money for a good cause.

HOLY WEEK AND EASTER

The sixth Sunday of Lent is known as **Palm Sunday** and it marks the beginning of **Holy Week**; the colour now is red. Before the Eucharist on Palm Sunday, there is a procession, if possible from outside the church, with all the people carrying palms or other branches, to celebrate Jesus' entry into Jerusalem. But in the church, the mood changes, and instead of a Gospel we hear the reading of the trial and passion of Jesus according to St Mark.

The Thursday of Holy Week is called **Maundy Thursday**, and the colour of the vestments today is white, the colour of celebration. The word 'Maundy' comes from the Latin 'mandatum', which means 'commandment'; on this day Jesus commanded his disciples to love one another, and also gave us the sacrament of the Eucharist. After the Gospel, some churches commemorate the washing of the disciples' feet by Jesus at the Last Supper, and after communion the president carries the Blessed Sacrament to a side altar where it will remain until Good Friday; he is accompanied by the servers carrying candles and perhaps by a thurifer. At the side altar a constant watch will be kept into the night as a re-enactment of Jesus' night in the Garden of Gethsemane. After the procession, the president and servers return to the sanctuary, and the altar hangings are stripped and the ornaments removed; when that has all been done, the president, servers and choir depart without formality.

On **Good Friday**, the day when Jesus was crucified, the Eucharist is not celebrated; the main service instead may be the Liturgy. During the Ministry of the Word of the Liturgy, the Passion from St John's Gospel is read or sung. Then a crucifix may be brought into the church by the president, accompanied by the servers with candles. The congregation are invited to show their love of Jesus by kneeling before the cross and kissing it; the servers may be required to hold the crucifix during the veneration. After this the Blessed Sacrament may be brought from the side altar and communion given. It is usual on Good Friday to genuflect to the crucifix when leaving the church.

There is no Eucharist on **Holy Saturday** either, but sometimes the first Eucharist of Easter is celebrated on the Saturday night. This follows the **Easter Vigil**, when as a sign of Jesus' resurrection new fire is struck and the **Easter candle** lit and brought into the church. In the vigil, the deacon, if there is one, sings the Paschal Proclamation of the salvation brought by the death and resurrection of Jesus, and there are a number of readings from the Old Testament pointing towards the events of Easter. Then the Gloria in Excelsis is sung and the Easter celebration begins. During the Eucharist, baptisms may take place, and all renew the promises made at their baptism. The vestments are always white or gold, as Easter is the most important and joyful festival of the Church, and the white vestments and hangings remain until Pentecost.

ASCENSION DAY ONWARDS

Ascension Day falls on a Thursday and is the day when the Church remembers how Jesus was taken into heaven. Ten days later is **Pentecost**, sometimes called Whit Sunday, the day when the young Church received the gift of the Holy Spirit. Red vestments are used today, because the Spirit appeared as flames of fire, and at **Confirmations**, when the Spirit is given as the seal of baptism. Feasts of **martyrs** also use red vestments and hangings, as red is the colour of blood; but on other **saints' days**, the colour is white.

As many as twenty-three Sundays after Pentecost follow, when the colour is usually green. The first Sunday after Pentecost, however, is known as **Trinity Sunday**, and the colour of the hangings is white. Each Sunday has its own theme, and the collect and the readings illustrate one aspect of the Gospel and of Jesus' life and teaching; careful attention will help our celebration of the Eucharist, and in our worship bring us closer to God.